the same-different

WINNER OF THE WALT WHITMAN AWARD FOR 2014

Sponsored by the Academy of American Poets, the Walt Whitman Award is given annually to the winner of an open competition among American poets who have not yet published a book of poems.

Judge for 2014: Rae Armantrout

the same-different

POEMS

HANNAH SANGHEE PARK

Louisiana State University Press | Baton Rouge

Published by Louisiana State University Press
Copyright © 2015 by Hannah Sanghee Park
All rights reserved
Manufactured in the United States of America
LSU Press Paperback Original
First printing

Designer: Michelle A. Neustrom
Typeface: Newslab

Thank you to the editors of the following journals and publications in which
these poems, or earlier versions of them, originally appeared: *32 Poems*:
"Bang"; *Anti-*: "Another Truth"; *DIAGRAM*: "Strip"; *PEN Poetry Series*: "Because
desire won't shrug off . . . ," "Sky the color of being photocopied too many times
. . . ," "Some History of Calamity," "I tell you I am scared of the dark, . . ." and
"Will you pull yourself together . . ."; *Poetry*: "And a Lie," "The Fox Bead in May,"
and "Norroway in February"; *Poetry Northwest*: "And A Lie," "One Truth," "Ps
& Qs," and "That Day"; *Poets.org*: "Nommo in September" and "Q"; *THERMOS*:
"Chiaroscuro/The First Day"; *Unsplendid*: "Ammit in March," "Dear Sir," "Qilin
in August," and "T/F"; *The Volta*: "The Same-Different." The poem "Bang" was
reprinted in *Best New Poets 2013*. The poem "One Truth" was reprinted in
Poetry Daily.

Library of Congress Cataloging-in-Publication Data
Park, Hannah Sanghee, 1986–
   [Poems. Selections.]
   The same-different : poems / Hannah Sanghee Park.
     pages cm
   Includes bibliographical references.
   ISBN 978-0-8071-6009-1 (pbk. : alk. paper) — ISBN 978-0-8071-6010-7
(pdf) — ISBN 978-0-8071-6011-4 (epub) — ISBN 978-0-8071-6012-1 (mobi)
   I. Title.
   PS3616.A74344A6 2015
   811'.6—dc23

                2014036091

For my mother and father, for everything—

Contents

I. The Same-Different

The barest word be what I say in you.
  —Merrill

You loved me. And your lies had their own probity.
  There was a truth in every falsehood.
   —Tsvetaeva

. . . the same—different—the same attributes,
different yet the same as before.
  —H. D.

Bang

Just what they said about the river:
rift and ever.

And nothing was left for the ether
there either.

And if anything below could mature:
a matter of nature.

It may have been holy as scripture
as scribes capture

meaning all that was there and only
(one and lonely)

is all that is left, and wholly
whose folly.

The sky bleached to cleanly
clear, evenly

to have left the world,
to what is left of it—

could you have anything left to covet?
Covertly met: coverlet. Clover, bet. Come over et—

Another Truth

I hungered on an
island. I'll end
whatever you want.

I'll want whatever
you ended on. It
was a lie, but I'll

take it. I tell you
half-truths. I whitely
lie while you ask

of me, you ask of
me too much. I take
it you agree.

I answer your questions with
questions. I question your answers.

And a Lie

The asking was askance.
And the tell all told.
So then, in tandem

anathema, and anthem.
The truth was on hold,
seeking too tasking.

And the wool was pulled
over as cover.
No eyes were kept peeled.

My iris I missed
the truth, now mistrust
all things seen, and this

distrust, the sounded distress signal
called and called and culled from your damsel.

One Truth

You say: evasive,
it won't hold water,
a sieve vs. vase

vis-à-vis I've saved
all the best truths
for this (the truth) a

nightlong longing for
a night of lying
with you. I do the

next best thing: a glance
(glancing) (it contains
all I want to contain).

Forgive the shy, the away. If
truth be told, I can't be true.

And A Lie

I'll take the untrue,
the tried and true, the ruing
the ruining. And you?

Rocks: the undoing.
Sea: the over and ever.
The lava stewing

its wet fire severs
the land and we love it.
We are made to fever

after a close fit.
He who made his living lying
through his teeth, his wit—

oh I know every truth was trying.
He who made his bed and lied in it.

T/F

It is the long con,
the construct of it.
You are always on:

Magnet and dragnet.
No use avoiding
the obvious us.

We live on a wing
and a prayer, thus:
first cry foul, then wolf.

I have so much bad
faith in our future
I don't know what to do.

This statement is false.
This falsity true.

P's & Q's

To dodge the question:
the query parried

back. An underrated
art, to thwart potential

quarrels, quandary
pared to quell and

awry, quarry pursued
if only to pursue.

An artful quibble.
Making the piddling

artless. Trade quip for
pun, quiz for puzzle,

puzzled for quizzical until the pittance.
To quit pitting against a quittance.

Strip

Like a frame within a frame the fossil
carried a carcass, a carapace,

and its own casket in another casket,
its own natural sarcophagus.

I never told anyone this story:
in a summer like this I ate a nectarine

until its rough corduroy pit, continued
rolling and chewing it until it hinged

open, and an inert spider, sitting
in white wisp, was inside like a small jewel.

How does a thing feel real. The layers
comprising me are, reductively, soft

hard, soft, an easy sift to the truth
but the hard sell and swallow done anyway.

In Flight

Some days I felt volant, as opposed to
a vole, an ant, things committed to dirt,

committed to crawl and burrow below.
This is no life for me. And neither stroll,

nor streets. The way I saw it, was a yaw:
the y-axis mine to mind, as if the wings

would, like months of proven frozen earth,
yield sudden shoots saluting a miracle.

My scapulae already provocative:
they provide vocatives at their unveiling.

The way you would, as you saw it, just sigh
at the sight of them. As if this could, alone,

shoulder the burden of your flight, as if
the back labor broke in was breaking for you.

That Day

One seed fanged its egg-tooth from its burred
and buried parcel, stirring hibernation.
Exhibiting green, and then high pronation:
its heart-shaped verdure arrowed downward.

It just gave up. Perhaps it saw its shadow
or winter's daunting windrows: white shoulders
of thinning streets, howling wind as poltergeist,
preferred potted earth to the iced meadow.

So when I upset the soil to find more
quitters, I mistook another seed's root
for sprout, corrected route to put it right

-side up, its thin wick waving its surrender.
Then surrendered. I blamed the sun's hot output,
but it had righted, rooted itself out of sight.

Telling Time

As ash rust was washed
watershed was marked.

We watched as daybreak
broke down into dark.

Noon regrew its head
until moon, then moon

starved it back. Daily
the daylily bloomed.

Others dallied for
an evening open:

the yellow evening
primrose knew no when.

Time hooped in the trunk's
orbiting to obit

when the ash took in the axe
and was meted by it.

Chiaroscuro/The First Day

A lung of light collapses
lightly along a

wall held with it.
While it withheld

your face from something soft,
something from your face oft-

en reads its own way.
And it's read one way,

it seems: sight unseen,
it's seen unsightly. See

the dark, necessary to undercut.
Cut to: darkness under the essay

of autumn atoming off via leaf.
Often, atonement leaves us

so compartmentalized (light from dark).
So come part me, light from dark

and breathe from it
and from it, breath.

No Man Is an Island

meaning he, it, the whole of it won't pass
un-tolled, untold. Meaning I AM NOMAN

on your island of no men, and what passes
as hospitality. I am No Name,

who would not exact me, who would not pass
across the lie of your lips. No-man's-land

I have left, with no more men who will pass
into the monster. Island of no name

except what roams you, ebb into your pass.
Thus THAT DAY AND HOUR KNOWETH NO MAN,

who said HEAVEN AND EARTH SHALL PASS AWAY,
exist to exit, date now dated, no man, no,

NOT THE ANGELS OF HEAVEN. No past, passed on,
now passé. From dust. And the exodus—

You Dear Specter—

I was steadfast, meaning
in your stead I fasted.

I drank from a sea collared
with wear. I lasted

as is, on an oasis.
I lived on the sand,

on its solid, liquid forms:
preservative and

purifier. Used to wound
it tight, or tighten wounds.

It should have kept for a while.
But the while was soon,

was sown, to bear no beck-and-call-you-later.
Thus remaining, instead, your dear spectator.

Dear Sir—

Two things
to think about.

Desire:
sires Eris,

ire.
On longing:

ongoing
log: *I long.*

Know nothing's worth
the strife and fire.

The end as un—
the on and on.

Some History of Calamity

Calamity thinned to calm | amity

Inside calamity, Alamo | city

Claim I jump and then calamity

Claim my city | I call it my own

Calamity Jane: a camp follower

Camp follower broken to   camp folk | lower

in rank than soldiers   Sweet skinner of mules

Tin cup of whiskey, bullwhacker, buckskin

Torn | fire, arranged: frontier   cause for celebrity

Celebrity being   cause célèbre | calamity

of the Great Plains   calamity by name   plain jane if

          by name   call me calamity

ROME

          Campo de' Fiori | *field of flowers*

Filled of followers   Bruno burns on   Tender tinder

, fled of followers   Calamity flowers   End in red din

INFERNO | calamity

Roma　　　On fire

Nero　　　No finer | Non-fire

Nero | *FIN*
(on fire)

On burns Bruno at the stake

FORMULA

Hearth | heat　　earth | at her | heart | heat at

then he | then *heathen* | heaven, then.

FORMULA

Feral flare | Fire, rife | Ni. Flamel in flame | infer no fear

On burns Bruno at the stake

Who wept to see

As he's | ashes
As his | ash is

swept to sea—

Shift

Taproot thirsted,
hurting for it.

Some days I can
conjure up your

scent, wilding me.
Sun-thawed snow a

doily on the
meadow. Starling

goes wild at my
whistling, oiled head

examining
all possible

points. The wind tucked
the leaves into roots

in hasty cleanup.
Wind tuning trees

together. I
meant everything when

and in this weather,
but isn't it wasted

when you don't need a
reason to stay? You

looked: spring squinting through
the earth, little glimpsed

greening.

Q

May I master love, undo its luster
do in the thing that makes us lust?

May I speed through the body's sinew
to marrow? Or is toiling a part of

the gaining of trust? May I pare and narrow
your body down, and open it to my

cupidity's arrow? May I find my
response to body's unanswered call

(if the want leaves you wanting, at all)?

&A

Being a matter
of importance, there

is no mastering
this but to bind you,

thrash and all, to the
mast. O you won't reach

irresistible song,
but the rope will teach

you the body's give.
Go down to the bone,

then tell me again
there what matters. It

will give you every
-thing you need to know

about what I cannot tell you and then,
just maybe then, could it be enough.

The Same-Different

Bared all, or barred all
depending on depth.

Sky a rerun of
yesterday's mixed sky.

But these days I take
what I can get, if

the getting was good.
Like a pure mirror

periodically
draped, could read/could not

read, would reveal/would
not, leaving with *We're*

a lot alike, meaning: O love, a love
I loved, and the lot I liked.

II. A Mutability

Narcissus in January

Already daffodils begin, their shoots
rabbit-ear out of soil packed by winter.

I call it. Perianth and corona
before March, a tilting cup and saucer.

Outer ring an offering (myself to),
inner ring an erring (I have stayed too

long after). I have stayed to long after
projected love; I may have made hay while

no sun shone and when it, pure pouring, shone
I whiled away while. I withered away,

and weigh the sum of stem and blossom, plus
or minus my reflection's heft—it was

the undoing, it was all I had else the man,
and the water's surface where we end, ends me.

Norroway in February

The glassy hill I clomb for thee

For sure-footed step, hooves behoove the haver.
The sky redid blue, the woman wavered,

and the black bull (the vanquisher) vanished.
She called out to nothing, and in vain shed

tears until she reached the glass hill's impasse.
Served her standard fairy-tale penance, *passim*,

served her seven to be given iron
shoes to—at last—scale the hill, the earned

neared end. Each step conquered territory,
at last, the sleeping prince-once-bull, torrid tearing

of clothes, tearing on one's clothes, three nights of this
until the prince awakes. How she, exhausted,

must have felt in the at long last, the ever after.
Happily, I guess, but a long time until laughter.

Ammit in March

It is *The Weighing of the Heart* (the left
pan) against an upright feather (right pan),
the plumb bob steadied, studied. If the heft

of the heart is considerable, and
hoists the feather up, know that it was sin
that sunk it. Below, Ammit hungers for hand-

led hearts, the kind that were damaged in
the bodily hunt: the want of what's not
yours, the kind that break, and those that broke in—

kind. Her crocodile head holds cold-blooded thoughts.
The hippopotamus back stamps for blood.
The only hope being her front: it's taught

that what comes in like a lion, like her, goes out
a lamb, and only by this mercy hearts reroute.

Baba Yaga in April

The month we met my mortar anchored me:
I only let you see my higher parts.
Nesting doll, vestal virgin, my pestle
sweeping back skeletons: say, past control.
My home is mobile: if I sing to it
the domicile turns docile, and offers
entry. The legs belong to the Black Stars,
the Barred Rocks, whatever pecks in the coop.
This is my baggage, what I do to dissuade
you. By one touch did you disarm me: that
was the moment; that was the moment I
took caution, halved it, and threw one half to
the wind. But see, I have loved you stupid.
I have sung my door open, for good.

The Fox Bead in May

The kiss is, strictly speaking, a passing
of of twice: a bead from her mouth to his,
then back, ad nauseam, and the boys who lived
and died for it. The lovely girl amassing

ninety-nine spirits, and in high spirits
for consuming her highest amount. Once
the hundredth boy arrived she starts her hunt
in her haunt, a hill's field filled with fitting

artemisia absinthium.
And every day they kissed to swap the bead
and for a month he waned and wans,

and when he learned the truth about her tongue,
he downed the bead: her true form a nine-tailed
fox who could have turned human, had he kissed on.

The Ensorcelled Prince in June

I reverse the men to fish.
I turned them colors.

Sank the city in water.
Bulked up islands to

mountains. And my lot in life,
so loathed, half of him

now stone. The other half so
human he can't stand

it. I love a better man,
half-dead. We lived on rats

and rags, but I could call it
love. Skin the thing. To absolution.

The half-statue half-killed him. Made his grave.
I flay the stone in him, the human of him.

Naga in July

I do not mind your many headed splendor,
your many hooded faces. If it is

love, it is love. If it is love we name
it by its many headed mane. At times,

I admit, I do not know where you cease
into scales, where your body joins and coils

its partings into one uninterrupted
unit. But these days even venom moves me

into the unspeakable. Expecting
nectar, not the hidden shift from human.

All monsoon season, letters repeated
in your absence. Left a ghost's husk of skin

you'd long outgrown, a tunnel of O's as the trail
to trace back, knowing: this is the hide that I seek.

Qilin in August

You who knew fervor, of its forever,
of its endless arch towards another's fevered
need. So I asked you, over and over,
sever me, sever me. What's heavier

than an unused heart, fat with its never-
seen potential? You who stilled a lover.
You who lived all your life with a cover.
Now it is August; now pull the lever.

What are you, honey, half-past the truth,
and made into myth. You've gone mythic on
me: dragon, unicorn, et cetera.
The auspice was suspect. I want some proof
there's luck to be ushered in, and when it's gone
I want to pull the cord on this era.

Nommo in September

There you exist in water.
Unending sketch and erase

of waves on the sea surface.
Today, you'll be all the words

I wanted to say: look, they're so
pretty in that second they

surface. You almost didn't
see them. You didn't see them.

Sinuous, so commitment's
a strange shape to hold and take.

I loved the water of you, the snake of
you, everything amorphous and short-lived,

as I expected nothing to last of us.
But when the waves break I still call them by name.

The Jackalope in October

Hoax or pox? How you come to me unknown.
    Trick and treat. This will require belief.
This will require treatment. On your feet.
    Feet of luck, well-wished upon. You were born

in the Year of the Rabbit, and what do
    you do? Enter myth. Enter tourist traps:
with your slapped-on pair of antlers. They clash
    with your essence, whatever that is. You

dazzle and flummox. You were born to lie.
    You are mistaken. Maybe fall's bare-all
        schema gave you the horns, or the virus

has gotten into all of us, and I
    can take a tumor for a prong. When the tall
        tales came true, nothing became of us.

Nagual in November

Dead ringer, dead ringer, everyman,
noman, phantom someone loved to loss.
Shapes were aped: now you're the very man
to swap identities. To hell with costs

and costumes: child's play, acting, beneath
your skills for a life undercover.
I'm duped, and due for unending grief
by the form first took: someone's lover,

someone's rock, someone's ever-longing con.
Someone's jaguar, somewhat dog. But rabbit
was the shift I got: outfoxing season's
cusp, coquetries, and all my bad habits.

What did I love; which form in the end?
The ruse to arouse? The tender pretend?

The Deer Woman in December

Let me tell you where the human in me ends.
Below my ankles, it's all deer. No one
ever looks so low, and for that, they're done
for. I mine my men this way, all condemned.

"Yet may I by no means my wearied mind
draw from the deer." Once, I wore and confessed
Noli Me Tangere around my neck
until I gifted it to you, as the hind

in me gave out. That if I cannot have you,
your hands on me, again. That if a closer
look revealed the hooves. I could never win.

Your touch was all it took. Nothing to do
but now move on. No use aching over
something there that never did begin.

III. Fear

. . . and that I seek, like such a beast, with my little strength, such a beast, with nothing of its species left but fear and fury, no, the fury is past, nothing but fear, nothing of all its due but fear centupled, fear of its shadow, no, blind from birth, of sound then, if you like, we'll have that, one must have something, it's a pity, but there it is, fear of sound, fear of sounds, the sounds of beasts, the sounds of men, sounds in the daytime and sounds at night, that's enough, fear of sounds, all sounds, more or less, more or less fear . . .

　—Beckett

Preface to Fear/False Spring

Because—

Spring unpacks itself as: sprig, airing
and winter simplifies to wet.

It was fine to assume the following.
The logs wear temporary casts of frost

and ice. Then the lichen scabbing over.
Icicles hand down hindered winter

to ground without it. Began with shed to
end in thaw. Leaves leaving off to

end in leaf. Snow smocks blotched with mud.
But winter loitered. Returned with a dread

of leaving, armed with enough wind to knock
the nectar out of flowers, blooming blocked.

That night, I mistook first snow this month
                    for moths. Next morning,
every acre nacreous. Ceased unto me.
                    Then bounding—

Because desire won't shrug off,
and the heart begins to eat its stores
its substance—slowly, at first, and
sparingly—

        (but nothing's left to lose so it is downed).
    We have a thing here called hunger,
a feeling and an ache, want of want.

You could try it sometime if you like.

Sun drinks down its own day.
Dusk takes us to task.
Hath drunk so deep.

You could be forgiven for not knowing.
You could be forgiven for a lot of things.

Yet
it must be nice, what you have, which I can't
quite explain: no fear, no missing or attachment,
sleep.
                    Do you see what I mean?
Unlikely. I explain my kinds of fear to your smile.
The parabola of it widening with each one.
The fear of wilds, the fear of wild and wilder men.

So
I can see what you mean. *Fool*, you think,
coward, child. What world do I inhabit.

Only a world you inhibit.

                                    Do I
bring you down, my sheering off, my sharing
offhand?

Small talk as particulars, particulate matter.

Will you pull yourself together,
asked my bones of me, a simple request
I honored for some time, until I realized,
asking back: *Will you pull me together?*

Will your pull

Let's try a conversation.
                    Your limit to watching anything
is five minutes before you are disinclined.
At first I didn't believe it. But I do.
I can only hold you for so long.

I walked home in the storm
(home, I called it home)
and some lone animal's tracks
cut perpendicular my own.

Quiet admiration the

                    mountain range your knuckles make,

your fists before you knelt,
                    your hands balletic

I tell you I am scared of the dark.

Again you: *why?* and *how?* and *what company am I
keeping?*

       Only that of someone whose liver is
a lily, whose lover was a likeness
          in this light—come here, I'll show you—
everybody has a likeness,
       not so much a light.

         Milk-livered, meaning lacking
courage. Courage, meaning *coeur* and *rage*,
heart and heat, brass of character.

            Crown vetch
before gold on the ground.

                    I had been letting something beaked
and angry eat my liver.

                    Regrowth a little blacker.
                         So: I have a liver and a lover.
One I liked to destroy
One destroying me

It is not what you think it is

It is the first dream I have where you leave me

Not lily or milk-livered: meaning white, unspoiled

But rot and all these things that keep me awake at night

If I ruin one I rue in the other

But I am good at that

Heart a plague in itself.

Then I am your placeholder

Liver working OT
Heart on its TO

Because this is happening or isn't happening

Beyond the meadow, the horizon fails
to make a connection. The sun goes under.
Sunset color-coded: call it splendor.
The mountain's scalp is out today. All its trails

visible through osseous trees,
to fade in night's wash. Everybody ooh'd
over the fresh delivery of snow.
And soon fussed the grasses into frenzy.

Clear of
the window you looked.
At breakfast, Andrew says coyotes are fearful,
which makes them good survivors. I broke

in: *I believe it*. Exercise caution
as takeaway. This morning, the dawn
ate night down to its rind. I saw it.
As waking to a coyote's mangled whine.

So nothing stays. These brown, dead leaves are so
last season. For the trees, this is their MO
So nobody gives them the memo.

The takeaway: we are all out here only
for ourselves, which is a survival technique.
Making us animals then, that we should seek
our own hide's sake first before the lonely

and inevitable finish: last man standing
in the survival of the fittest, handing
what then to our victor's highest marks?
Only fear regrouping in your heart of hearts.

You can be any character
you like in my script. I suggest the role of the fool,
the coward, not as typecasting but a lesson
in relearning fear: to be feral. A lesson in living me.
A lesson for a second. A lesson for less than five
minutes of your time.

                              Metronome your heart

You check your watch.

                    It has a face and hands
Meaning:

        That's not why I lock my door.

I always used to leave my keys inside the lock,
the knob,
            for you to enter and break.
            By leaving it, I let it so

                    Now do you see?

O I don't expect you to.

My mouth a bivalve.

     I call your bluff,

I burrow marrow

    Without the help of the wind, your tulips,
     drooping, hate their bob cuts.
      I used to cut my hair
after hurt.
    (Fool)

   what am I after   locks.

My own, falling to my ribcage
and the ones that keep me.

    Ribcage a series of endless parentheses around the heart:

    again   again   again

        the point not made enough

  I lock my door because it's night.

The hinges of a door.

    It hinges on a door
to keep out and let in.

    It is like poor sleep.

You give me something for it.
You give me poor sleep.

If you look the right way, the snow's thick
shavings are houndstooth

                           but only at night.
I try to limit that   but only at night.

Night will have the floor, now
                           think of a black fog,
doing as all fogs do, undecided on what to
occupy: ground or sky

          whatever you wish.

something torn apart in the woods.

You don't know that.

          Skeleton as a way of asking someone else's miracle

          Hide as, to save your own.

          Hide as, I am doing that. I am saving my own

          Seek as: I will not always be here.

          You: I took no notice.

Our only commonality,
                the common cold.
Glabrous the leaves.
                Stark, scarce of valor.
Vale of tears it is to me.
                Valley of whatever
you choose to call it.
                As I see it,

the trees were goring the snow.

                They were the offenders.

I don't care if they were here all year.

                It is the only part that could not conceal.

I couldn't see it.

                I can't see you, meaning

I won't see you.

Mercy is a thing mastered,

                with a master

I ask of you your silence

                You:

          and you,   ,

                You—

The light flinches, and I fear.

As the snow heaped proportional to sheets,
trees balancing snow for some time,

then the universal gesture for giving up.

The snowplow darkens the road

There are runs in my stockings like plowed road,
revealing   a clearing.

I adore you. Am I to pretend otherwise.

Chaos as chase

We joke of thinned air,
leaked gas, breathing things
that only impair.

Now I think if I push a little bit harder you will stay.

Now I push a little bit harder.

Know I push a little bit harder.

Branches lidded with snow

The pelt ours for the taking

fare-thee-well
as farewell,
I fear thee well
I keep telling you
                    I keep letting you

but no less of it. Meaning.

Far from me, and the heart flares.
You might as well be. . . .

The pier was . . . special to me.
Now I do my liver in, for kicks.

So heart do right by me.

Tops of bare trees like overused paintbrushes

And what is one to do: have ease
have its way, or heave
against it. Tell me. Let me.

Sky the color of being photocopied too many times.

Then the coming sun boils off the sea's gray.

It is a fear of rejection.

Keeping my cards close.

Do what is needed   do you hear me?
Do what is needed.

So I feared.

River muscled through land.

There is a grace there in your neck

Things for my mouth:

    —A fig leaf
    —Desalination
    —So much soap

I watch my language: it seems to be doing OK.

It's only been a day, you say.

        A day plus a night.

I would ask so much but

           silence an answer in itself

Speak to me.

Silence fearful.

I will be good.

Heart the organ that speaks you.

Listen to me: you don't live with this mouth.

So let me go over this one last time
because departure means you will forget,
forgo the company of fear,

      the company of fools.

I amuse you for only so long.

So long—

to fear the past's grasp on the future.

Everything must and will come to its end.

This lovely creature,
     this space I am breathing and not breathing,

        will be taken from me.

Then everything in life is a placeholder.

   So—
   Would you go back then?
   And then—
   And then?

   Even then—and even then—
   —and even—even, then.

Acknowledgments

Love to my sister, Sarah, and my brothers, Daniel and Isaac.
My parents.

To the Academy of American Poets and Rae Armantrout, my deepest
gratitude and highest honor—thank you so much. LSU Press.

For their professional support, thank you to Don Share and The
Poetry Foundation. The USC School of Cinematic Arts, the Iowa
Writers' Workshop, and the University of Washington. 4Culture and
The Iowa Arts Council/National Endowment for the Arts. The Ful-
bright Program and my fellow fellows.

For The MacDowell Colony (where most of this book was written)—
thank you for pure heaven/haven. The gala-open studios group, for
their love, conversations, and brilliance—all owed and awed. Blake
Tewksbury.

Thank you to my professors for their tutelage and poetry over the
years, all of which was invaluable in living. My hero Cody Walker,
Dan Beachy-Quick, Linda Bierds, Mark Levine, and Jim Galvin (who
started this). For Rick Kenney: cortex, core, and text. All that a sound
can carry and a star can shoot.

Beloved Elizabeth Robinson, every word and still no words.

Patrick Brodie, my sonne. Jessica Pak. Alex Walton.

My hearts: Eleza Jaeger and Hil Jaeger. Vero Gonzalez and Lauren
Harrison. Jane Wong (who's that?). Ossian Foley. Taryn Schwilling.
Shreya Madhavaram.

Catherine Park and Klara Kim.

Gary Lee: a life of letters.

Jane Shim: as if life led to and from you—

Notes

"No Man Is an Island": The quotes are from Matthew 24:35–36 (KJV).

All the sonnets in Part II, "A Mutability," are rooted in myths, fairy tales, and folklore from different cultures. The titular characters are hybrids, chimeras, or shape-shifters.

"Narcissus in January": This is a story from the Greek myth of Narcissus, a man in love with his own reflection. He eventually turned into a daffodil.

"Norroway in February": This is a story from *The Black Bull of Norroway*, an English adaptation of a Scottish fairy tale. A young woman toils to find her love (a prince transformed into a bull). The epigraph is from the fairy tale—a line from the song she sings to him.

"Ammit in March": This is a story from the ancient Egyptian *Book of the Dead*. Ammit is an amalgam of a lion, hippopotamus, and a crocodile. She lives in the underworld and sits by the scales of justice, waiting to see if a person's heart is pure or not—and if not, she eats the heart and condemns the soul to wander forever.

"Baba Yaga in April": This is a story from Russian folklore. Baba Yaga is a witch who often travels around with her body wedged in a mortar, using a pestle to steer herself. Her hut is also mobile, as it possesses chicken legs.

"The Fox Bead in May": This is a story from *The Fox Bead*, a Korean folktale. The nine-tailed fox, or the gumiho can shape-shift into a beautiful young woman. She uses this disguise to eat the souls of young men to permanently become human.

"The Ensorcelled Prince in June": This is a story within a story—
"The Ensorcelled Prince" from "The Fisherman and the Jinnee" in
The Arabian Nights. It's from the perspective of the sorceress who
turned the prince into half a statue as punishment for half-killing
her lover. She also turned all the citizens into fish.

"Naga in July": This is a story from the ancient Indian *Mahabharata*.
Naga can refer to a specific king cobra deity (or all cobras) who can
take human form. They are usually associated with water, storms,
and both positive and negative forces.

"Qilin in August": This is a story from Chinese mythology. A qilin is
usually referred to as the Chinese unicorn, though it is commonly
depicted with two horns and is a hodge-podge of many animals,
most notably a dragon. It is said to bring good luck, and to see one is
a prosperous omen.

"Nommo in September": This is a creation story from the Dogon
people of Mali. In the popular version, the Nommo were spirits as-
sociated with water sent down to earth from the god Amma. In the
esoteric version, the Nommo came from the union of Amma and the
earth. They were aqueous and serpentine beings, similar to Nagas.
Their fluid characteristics were given to the Dogon ancestors, who
lost the trait by offending Amma.

"Jackalope in October": This is a story from American folklore. The
jackalope, a portmanteau of jackrabbit and antelope, is a horned
rabbit created as a joke that later became legend in the American
West. Earlier manifestations of this, as with all of these stories, have
been found in many different cultures. It is suspected that the leg-
end of a horned rabbit is simply a sighting of a rabbit infected with
Shope papilloma virus, a disease that produces cerebral tumors that
resemble horns.

"Nagual in November": This is a story from Mesoamerican folk-
lore. The Nagual is a person who can shape-shift into any animal it
chooses.

"The Deer Woman in December": This is a story from Native American myth. Many tribes have slight variations of The Deer Woman, a spirit who, similar to the gumiho, is a beautiful young woman who bewitches men and destroys them. Her only ruminant parts are her hooves. If the hooves are seen, the spell is broken, as her true self is revealed. The quoted lines are from Sir Thomas Wyatt's "Whoso List to Hunt, I Know where is an Hind."